Love the Albatross

Deborah Harvey

Indigo Dreams Publishing

First Edition: Love the Albatross
First published in Great Britain in 2024 by:
Indigo Dreams Publishing
24, Forest Houses
Cookworthy Moor
Halwill
Beaworthy
Devon
EX21 5UU
www.indigodreamspublishing.com

ISBN 978-1-912876-85-3

British Library Cataloguing in Publication Data. A CIP record for this book can be obtained from the British Library.

Designed and typeset in Palatino Linotype by Indigo Dreams.
Cover artwork and illustrations ©Katie Marland 2024.
Cover design by Ronnie Goodyer.
Printed and bound in Great Britain by 4edge Ltd.

Papers used by Indigo Dreams are recyclable products made from wood grown in sustainable forests following the guidance of the Forest Stewardship Council.

For Wisdom the Laysan albatross,
with admiration

Acknowledgements

Many thanks to the editors of the following journals, e-journals and anthologies, in which poems in this collection first appeared: *Abridged, Amsterdam Quarterly, Artemis Poetry, Atrium, Buzzwords, Caduceus, Crowstep Journal, Dream Catcher, Finished Creatures, Fragmented Voices, iamb ~ poetry seen and heard, Ink Sweat & Tears, London Grip, Night Sweats of the Spirit (Maitri Poetry), Obsessed with Pipework, Raceme, Rat's Ass Review, The Dawntreader, The Fig Tree, Ticking Clock (Frosted Fire).* Also, to Dawn Gorman and Peter O'Grady of West Wilts Radio's *The Poetry Place,* where some of these poems were first broadcast.

'Conversations with silence' won second prize in the 2022 Buzzwords Poetry Competition. 'Just when you get yourself out of one labyrinth' was short-listed for the 2023 Plough Poetry Prize, and highly commended in the 2024 Slipstream Poetry Competition, while 'No protocols can save me now' and 'Your silence is all I have left' were short-listed for the 2021 and 2023 Bridport Prize respectively, with the latter also winning a runner-up prize in the 2023 Frosted Fire Single Poem Competition. 'When an albatross crash-lands in a dream' was Ink Sweat & Tears' April 2023 Pick of the Month.

My gratitude also to Colin Brown of The Leaping Word and the poets of the Friday Morning Poetry Groups; and to Kim Moore, Helen Mort and my fellow students on the 2020 – 2022 Manchester Writing School MA in Creative Writing course.

CONTENTS

Part I

Part II

Part III

Love the Albatross

Estrangement Stories

When an albatross crash-lands in a dream

Long ago I saw an albatross fly
head-first into a dream so fast so

hard it penetrated half a mile deep.
Inside the crater

a wreckage of feather and bone
remains which over millennia became

this fossilised skull you've found and which
slicing open my right forearm

you press into the wound
holding the edges until they knit.

We'll keep this for later, you tell me
we'll talk about it then.

Part I

Love the Albatross

This emptiness
is not a lack of will or memory
nor is it a want of words, a deficit of feeling

it's more the loss of something
you maybe never had, though you love it
more than you love yourself.

(That you don't much love yourself
is not a comment on the quality of this other love
which is an albatross always

returning to its habitual nesting place
and freighted with all you know about albatrosses
and poetry.) It's also

this: how do you tell a story
when you don't know how it ends, which isn't
in your power or remit to shape

though maybe that's what you're doing right now
maybe these words are spurs or goads
maybe crossbow bolts.

The distance between us

There's a dance we've had to learn
in this time of plague
not just the age-old turn with death
hand in grasping bony hand
but skirting around each other
keeping a perfect space
alert to each shift like starlings
wheeling over reed beds.

And if our space predates this time
and if it lasts longer
does that also count as love,
this distance that makes us reframe ourselves
like trees whose rifts and hollows
offer up new sky?

No protocols can save me now

You were blue, they said, and they cut the cord
and whisked you away

returning you to my arms a more appropriate pink.
I held onto you tightly. And that was the first time.

On the second occasion it was you in charge of the scissors
and somehow you forgot to grab me sent me

whirling into space out of reach of everything
which is where I am still

with dwindling supplies of water and oxygen. Already
I've watched the sun set and rise enough times

to lose all novelty and
now, with the rest of my breath, I'll remember

that night, you and me tucked together on a trolley
pushed through corridors

the lamps wheeling over our heads
passing planets.

Thirteen ways to leave your mother

after Paul Simon

We might have stayed longer in the pub
but you popped to the toilet, locked yourself in,
climbed out through the window

We might have shopped till we dropped
but you slipped from the changing rooms in disguise
so I'd not recognise you

We might have had cream teas in a garden
but you set seed and made your escape along verges
through hedgerows

We might have learnt how to draw together
but you took a line for a walk that led
where I couldn't follow

We might have shelled walnuts and baked a cake
but you made a boat with a paper sail
I was too big to fit in

We might have watched cartoons on the telly
but when I drew a door in a wall of rock
you ran through it

We might have spent all day at the zoo
but you set loose the tigers, the kangaroos,
hitched a lift on an ostrich

We might have journeyed to the moon
but somehow the rocket took off too soon
stranding me on the launch pad

We might have wandered the length of the beach
but the tide was in flood, I got stuck in mud,
you kept on walking

We might have sat out the storm together
but gale force winds came roaring in, sucked you
up through the chimney

We might have held tightly to each other
but I've grown old, my hands are cold,
you slipped through my fingers

We might have written a happy ending
but I lost the words, you found it absurd, the plot
dropped through the grating

We might have stayed family till the end
but you typed a message and pressed send,
clicked on Block

Stay At Home

Stay At Home, they tell us
Protect the NHS
Save Lives

and I think of the girl I saw in town
six weeks earlier
surfacing to rain

then ducking back down in her sleeping bag
fishing for lipstick, a mirror,
crimsoning her mouth

Today she's breaking my heart again
and I think of you
in your white-walled room

if that's where you're living
if that's where you're safe

The last traces of Doggerland

Maybe this is what happened. Bulldozed by ice, the water that was our story began to spill over the ridge, eroding chalk slowly then faster & faster the rock broke open the valleys filled. And in the rush to save our truths we found ourselves on opposite sides of a widening gulf & while I was climbing a ladder & searching my pockets for a handkerchief to wave, you started speaking in a language I didn't understand, I couldn't hear you. Or maybe we were both carried off in its currents maybe mackerel and sea lice have fed on our meat & somewhere across this vast seabed my bones are searching for yours.

Beyond the pale

Or maybe it happens like this. You're in a queue so long it might stretch further than the moon but there's no chit-chat, no solidarity, everyone stays silent, staring at their shoes. From time to time a gap opens up & you all shuffle forward. When you reach the front, if you ever reach the front, you'll hold out your hand, await the ink stamp of unacceptability colour-coded according to infringement that not even Coca-Cola will wash off & then some colossus will step forward, seize each of you by the wrists, swing you in five full rotations above its head & let go, sending you flying over ramparts into distant tree-tops where you'll lodge like minor celestial bodies. Not one of you will have anything to shine about.

Losing everything on the M6 in the rain

There were hugs as you left
and you felt you'd largely been forgiven
for letting the cat slip out through your legs
as you carried in cardboard boxes and bags
the tortoiseshell queen taking her chance in a single
pea-green glance and gone
careless words off a careless tongue
and eight hours later you're driving home
a hundred and sixty miles in the rain
boot lock jammed open, lid flying up
and your backpack laptop papers
vanishing in the dark.

If that's what happened.
You know there were hugs as you left.
You felt you'd largely been forgiven
for letting the cat slip out through your legs
as you carried in cardboard boxes and bags
carelessly. There'd been a hunt. Words off a tongue.
She must have slipped out when you weren't watching
a shadow cat more black than bronze
and asleep on bin liners in the kitchen
where she'd been all along.

Forgiven — careless — you hugged
the drive home slow in the inside lane
boot lock jammed open, lid roped shut
and somewhere miles behind you
a key turning in a lock.

Once we were birds

A mother pelican wasn't something
I'd ever aspired to be
but there I was all the same, pecking and
pecking at my breast till it bled and my brood could feed.
Meanwhile your father was doing what male tits do
neglecting his nesting duties for extra-pair mating.

As for maternal ambition
I never hoped you'd be Uncle Noel's racing pigeon
the one he sold and sold and sold only for it to
head straight home
though each April and May when the swifts return
writing their journey over the sky, I wide-
open the window, let my longing
fly to greet them.

Part II

Fledglings

Another poem has chipped a hole
through its shell, just big enough for me
to glimpse damp exhaustion.

I can't make out what species it is
I've never learnt the calligraphy of eggs
though like the others, this poem will
eat what's offered
grow until it's strong enough to teeter on the brink
test both wings in a preliminary fluttering
and take flight.

If it turns out to be a robin
it will carve out its territory nearby
shouting threats over the garden fence
turning up on the doorstep each Christmas
black-beaked and beady.

If it's a chiffchaff or a swallow
it will insist it's all about the journey
not the arrival.

Maybe one day this poem will fly your way
a goose calling as it heads north
making for a land where the cold summer
sun never sets.

Starling Story

The day two starlings fell down the chimney and made
my sister scream and my parents thundered downstairs
and I followed and my father sent me back to my room
so I never saw starlings or my sister's terror or my
mother's vexation, and had no part in this story that's my
family's story and the starlings' story —

yes, that was the day I knew I'd always be at the edge of
things

though later that morning
when I looked up

I read what they'd written on the ceiling
with their panicked sooty wings

and understood it.

What the currents of the Skagerrak taught me

By the time the bottle
I'd lobbed into the middle of the North Sea
washed up on a beach in Frederikshavn
and the person who found it told the local paper
and letters written in fluent English by ten-year-old
Danish girls deluged my parents' doormat
I'd long grown out of
ponies, popstars and penfriends

but what astonished me then
comforts me now
the convolution of tidal cycles
the push and pull of wind and moon
the notion that nothing we leave behind us
is gone forever.

Messages from the other side

During the fourth month of our acquaintance
you started writing messages
from the other side

fluttering movements at first
that became an urgent jabbing shorthand
showing purple through my skin.

The volume of these communications
made a junior doctor gasp
but I was intent only on their meaning

how this time we should get it right
make a pact before we forget and I
dwindle into your mother, you

subside into my child and we
no longer hear ourselves talking
in our other home.

Small hours

The voice I don't hear stops me
dead in my sleep

the street lamp at the window
throwing shadows that remember

the prickle and shiver from bed to cradle
the orange light of the radiator

just enough to read your face for a hint of
who you were, what you might be thinking.

Meanwhile the rest of the house the street the whole
city was asleep

everyone but you and me and my sisters out there
somewhere in the dark

moon-faced in washed-out dressing gowns
their babies stirring in their arms

each of us trying to decipher
the same code.

And I have to wonder all these years later
if it's just me who waits alone

longing for words that stay unspoken
love that won't be shown.

Premonition

It was early September
and we were living in a city
on the far side of the country.

I knew no one
and when people heard me speak they'd say don't tell me,
you're from Norfolk. (I'd never been to Norfolk.)

One day I was pushing you in your pushchair
through the park and there was this bite in the air, the first
shiver of winter

and it took me back to the year before
when we lived closer to home and I was
carrying you under my ribs

never having seen your face
or rested my cheek on the curve of your head, just
waiting for you, the dream of you, the

love of you.
The loneliness I felt that day
is the same I carry everywhere with me

now you're ten years older than I was then
and living in a city
at the far end of the country.

Her albatross years

The changes were manageable to begin with
but when feathers stubbled the skin of her shoulders
she tried to push them back in, she didn't want to be

an Angel or Madonna of the Atypical Offspring
but the choice was already out of what were no longer her
hands but pinions at the end of cambered wings.

She squinted at where her nose used to be
glimpsed instead a hooked pink beak
but it was only when she found herself wind-

flung, an ocean away
from where she'd hoped to be
that she realised they'd made of her an albatross

the one bird that will always fly those extra ten
thousand miles and never need help or even sleep.
Years passed and eventually

she bargained herself down to herring gull status
hung her vast wings at the back of the wardrobe
and learnt how to steal cheese and pickle sandwiches

from unwary tourists. Few of the mates
she hangs out with now know of her albatross years
and those who do have all but forgotten, it's only

you who'd still pin her
up there, wings locked as she glides air masses
her heart barely beating.

Just when you get yourself out of one labyrinth

you find you're in another, in fact, you're not only in it,
you're accidentally helping to build it & trapping your
children inside with you where you can't keep them safe,
I know, what a ridiculous promise that was. It's the exits
that are entrances that are the problem, they're so
difficult to spot & since the story starts with you already
inside, you'll have to think backwards. Maybe it's that
stone staircase that tunnels down, getting narrower with
each step, till you squeeze into a room with walls the
colour of smokers' lungs, bare lightbulbs & abandoned
fridges, where the glass in the portholes is reinforced
with grids of wire. Or perhaps it's that chute you saw in
the museum of a coastal town, or maybe it was London,
anyhow, it's the same neighbourhood where a serial
killer's operating by means of secret passages through
cellars & the guide says of course we're not going down
there & gives you a shove & you find yourself wedged
between brick walls, dangling over a long drop into
nothing. Or perhaps it's the aperture of a shell that's the
whorl of your newborn's ear & you're clattering round &
round its spiral steps, desperate to find them & bring
them out & you run through rooms to get to rooms to get
to the one room in the house you'd forgotten about,
where the creature who was there all along steps from
the darkness & turns to face you, a shape in the mirror.

When a story can't see a way out

A week after our family story
jumped from the balcony of its flat
I sat on the doorstep. A line
half-way between up there and
down here had been crossed
and nothing was unthinkable any more.

From its perch in the pear tree
a blackbird was singing
shackles
chains around my feet
and even the swifts were anchors
weighing down the sky.

Disappointment is a sedimentary rock

It's impossible to know
how long the process takes
(she's underground, sees no seasons
or phases of the moon)
but it's long enough for her to slough
all her existing body hair, grow whiskers on her face,
bristles between her toes.
Her teeth have changed too:
longer now, they move
independently of each other, like chopsticks
so she throws away her spade
and shears soil with them instead.
Sometimes males dig long straight
tunnels towards her but she ignores them.
She is fossorial, aggressive,
surprisingly long-lived.

The red thread

The first time I saw our story
it was standing in a meadow outside Throwleigh

its steaming coat the colour of rust, in shape and size
not unlike an eight-berth static caravan

and I noticed it had noticed us, was watching us
through eyes that were small and mean

as we clustered together, tried to make ourselves bigger
than it thought it was.

Stumbling up the track I spotted a gap
where a gate was missing and pulled you through

as if it couldn't follow, as if somehow
this would keep us safe.

Glancing back
I saw it snort in freezing air.

When I opened the cage of my fingers
to let you fly

I never thought you'd return for good
but kept my hand out-

stretched all the same, to offer
a perching place when you flew past.

For a few years you'd drop by
feathered with stories

but over time those fly-
pasts came to a stop

the joints in my fingers started to knot
my whole arm stiffened.

Now my mouth is full of wood
sap blinds my eyes

the rain that weighs on my leaves
the steady drip of loss.

Subsong

When the last of the fledglings are gone
the parent blackbirds also vanish
into the depths of the underbrush
where they hunch, unnoticed,
for as long as recuperation takes.

They're not there to repent
or to consider the ways
they might have done things better
picking over each act for a lack
of thought or kindliness

but perhaps they won't mind
if I sit beside them
wait it out in this homely dark
shedding disappointments oh so many
broken feathers.

When love isn't the answer

When the box I'd sent you came back marked Not Known At This Address I was at a loss. I'd moved to a smaller house, the spare room was crammed with your brother's belongings & opening the shed door would likely trigger an avalanche. Meanwhile the love packed inside it was gorging on hunger, doubling in size, threatening to burst from its container. In the end I opened it anyway & broke off a piece to feed to the dog but he was turning into part of the landscape the way old collies do & when I offered it to your sister & brothers they said they had plenty already, thanks, Mum. As for foisting it on your grandmother, that was a non-starter, she was busy off-loading everything I'd ever given her like there was no tomorrow, which turned out to be largely true. Besides it was your name running through it, if I smashed it into a thousand pieces every splinter would make its way back to you. In the end I stuck the box up with tape, stuck it up in the attic. At night I hear sounds that might be creaking, might be thunder & lightning, might be this house, its foundations subsiding.

A family history of refractive errors

Tell me about your mother
the therapist said

and I stared at the floor, unsure how to start
all I could see was the grain of her skin
the knot of her nose, cherry pink
lipstick smeared on a tooth

It took me years to look past the wood
focus on tree

Now I've climbed to the top to take in the view
only to spot our distance
running at twice the speed of silence
over the clouded horizon

Is our gap wide enough now?

If I dress in hi-vis and wave both my arms,
do you think you might see me?

Heart failure

Two days is the longest you can get away with
before your aunt tells you your mother tells her
she never sees you.

Though in fact, it's not that much of a burden
only an hour or so after work
plus driving her to church and back on Sunday
and shepherding her through the aisles of Lidl
every Saturday morning for Rich Tea biscuits
a box of Kellogg's cornflakes
two packs of Tena Lady
and the Daily Mail.

She's stopped knitting baby coats and bed socks
now it's Christmas pudding hats all year round.
You bring her more wool:
green for holly leaves, scarlet for berries
though that green's too dark, she says
you should have got emerald.
Sometimes when she's breathless
her lips look mauve.

She asks you your news but carries on talking.
How the Bears scored six tries last night
though the ref still lost them the match
and Edith's had another fall
and you know Marion who sits in the pew in front, well
her son's just found out the baby isn't his after all
his wife's gone off with the real father
and taken the little one with her
and Marion won't have to mind him anymore
she's broken-hearted.

Back home you write down
the other things she says
so you won't gloss over them
at some unspecified point in the future
when you find yourself
face-to-face with a box of tissues and
someone who listens.

You google the end stages of heart failure
learn you've visited this page many times.

How to manage tidal surge and coastal erosion

Method I

Sitting outside her house in my car
I picture a concrete wall with a curved lip

that turns the energy of each wave
back on itself.

After a few minutes I too am
smooth, hard and grey

there's nothing to latch onto
nowhere for anything to stick.

I've come late to this technique
and she is pent, she's fretting in her armchair

as I open the back door, call through the hatch
put the kettle on to boil

and all the water that makes up my mother
begins to simmer and seethe.

Method II

You saw the lie of the land earlier than I did.
Maybe you were already grading sediments at school

gluing mud particles with algae in the science lab
and selecting pioneer plants —

cord grass, and glasswort that turns crimson
every autumn.

What's more, you worked quickly, single-mindedly.
Before I knew it, your salt marsh was vast

and acres of sea aster sea lettuce sea lavender
stretched between us.

Now I'm far enough away to be invisible.
If I run I might sink to my waist.

If I send up a flare
only peewits and curlews are likely to see it.

When a story loses the plot

And then there's the part of the story
that stays in the swelter of the labyrinth
reading from an old and now
discredited script.

It doesn't know it's dead
and the rest of it has moved on
but that doesn't matter, you're

here to sit with it, hold the darkness
stroke its neck, its horns, its head.

Part III

Here be dragons

In its larval form, a newly-hatched poem, known as an 'inkling' or 'intimation', can live beneath the surface, in the mud of the mind, for anything from a few months to five years. Propelled by farting & with mouthparts like excavator buckets, they're uniformly repulsive until the moment they write themselves out of their skins & become something visionary or even unearthly. Over the years I've watched many of them complete their life-cycle but lately something untoward has been happening & instead of dispersing to hawk riverbanks & byways, searching for readers to prey on, they've been buzzing at my window, battering their helmets against the glass, as if they might break in, as if they've come back to bite me.

Birdsong with chainsaw

I'd come to think of it as mine
on evenings silenced by the moon

when I'd watch from the window
try to unravel its knotted branches

or at the equinox, as the migrant sun
swam north and south to its return

snagging in its net like a salmon
coming home to spawn

due East defined by the fall of light through
mossy trellises and later yellowing leaves

and taken for granted till the dawn
I see the ash tree is gone

and the sound I'd blotted out
takes shape in empty sky.

On ice

'There are years that ask questions and years that answer'
Zora Neale Hurston

Did this longest silence
begin in a year that asked questions?

It's so long ago it's hard to be sure but I don't
recall there being more than those times

when your silences were shorter though
sharper perhaps, because surely time must blunt their edges?

There's a question. And now I think of it
maybe all the years that have followed have asked questions

too, look, they're piling up in drifts, an endless
snowfield smothering every struggling answer.

Radio silence

James Burke crosses his fingers
Cliff Michelmore's chewing his nails
even my father heaves a sigh
says he reckons that's it

while I'm aghast at the failure of grown-ups
the doing nothing, this stifling
silence until life comes crackling back and the scientists
at Mission Control start to cheer and clap.

And now here I am, more than fifty years later
not sitting in my car outside my child's last known address
not going to the places I think they'd go
not buying a new phone that could evade their defences.

All I do is wait (though waiting feels pointless)
and listen through radio silence for a sign of life.

There's a kind of sadness

that escapes through my nose and mouth
in the night and blinds the windows.

I swab them dry each morning with an old towel
but it's always there the next day.

It settles on skirting boards too, thick enough
to write your name in, solidifies under sofas and chairs.

Sometimes I forget to watch where I'm going
and stub my toe on it.

When it first turned up I wanted nothing to do with it —
to be honest I'd had it up to

here with grief — yet somehow it found
an empty parking space right outside my front door.

For months I walked past it, eyes averted,
but it soon became clear it wasn't going anywhere

so each year on your birthday
I make it a cake

and set a place for it at the table for Christmas dinner.
On Mother's Day I buy it flowers.

I think over time it's got used to me too. At night
it jumps on my bed, curls up snug in the crook of my knees and

by morning it's sound asleep on my head, we've finally learnt
we're all we've got.

Conversations with silence

i

Silence arrives like a starling
hitting a window

It isn't eloquent or pregnant

It allows you to take its coat
but waves away your offer
of a cup of tea

There's no point
trying to curry favour, it says
We're not here to ingratiate ourselves
or make friends

It sits down
stares straight ahead

There's nothing golden about it
plenty that is guilt

ii

You know where silence lives
under the roots of conifers

how it lies on the roofs of garden sheds
sunning itself on the shortest day

when it breeds other silences
that romp in gardens
squeeze through holes in fences
bare teeth that catch the light
one night when you swing into the street
to find it waiting at the top of the lane
fully-grown

how it stares down you and the dog

trots a few yards into shadow, turns
and waits

iii

There's no such thing as silence
silence tells you

Even when birds are mute and traffic stilled
the lack of noise keeps screeching
shrill, and silvery as dace

At night it darts through the labyrinth
sprints the length of the canal
ricocheting under bridges
and off surfaces

And you've only
yourself to blame, silence adds
It was you who struck the bell with that hammer

Now it's getting louder and louder
the walls are cracking

iv

There was this silence, sitting on the pub wall
holding a bag of crisps

Cars went past, the drivers and passengers
oblivious to it waiting there, small and dark, in a cardigan
and sandals, legs swinging, eating crisps

Passers-by might have felt a slight chill in the air
but barely enough to draw their attention so it didn't
they were busy having a laugh it was summer it was
Friday night for Christ's sake

Only the dog that belonged to no one
that could also evade attention
noticed the silence, trotted over, licked a hand

The silence gave it a crisp
The dog ate it without a sound

v

If silence wore glasses
it would look
over the top of them
and tell you to pick up a pen
write it all down
but it has no eyes
no nose to balance them on
and no mouth either —

it is silence, after all —

and anyway
you don't have a hand free
you're too busy
lugging silence around like it's
all you have left

vi

Your mother thought silence was a kitten
to be drowned in words

As soon as she left
you'd haul it out
hold it up by the hind legs
and breathe air into its nose
then rub it dry and tuck it into your coat

Who knows if it remembers
how often you saved its life
now it's fully grown
and one pat of its steel-clawed paw
would cause considerable damage

one bite through the back of your neck
would be the end

vii

You type a few words, highlight
and delete them
The screen looks at you
blankly

The page is white
but not as white as if they'd
never been set down

something of your impulse lingers

just as the silence that follows a name
is not the same as the silence
that existed before it

that's changed for ever
by what's no longer heard

You saw the geese fly over
you read the marks they left on the air

When a story seeks validation

Somehow you're in an unknown country
dressed in white with a sash of red
and you're running through streets
that are narrow, paved with slippery cobbles

and the blood in your skull is pounding
the slither and thud of hooves are pounding
through deadening heat, a smother of dust
blistering breath on the back of your neck and you

daren't look behind you to where
your story is scattering grievances and wants
in a herd of identical narratives
chasing their chosen conclusion.

51°16'17N   3°1'24W

Today I took you to the beach.
We parked beyond the row of bungalows
where that woman stabbed her husband over
bubble and squeak, and followed the footpath
that starts in the churchyard
tunnelling through buckthorn to the sea.

As we skirted the big yellow buoy roped to the wreck
where you sat and smoked a roll-up
that last Christmas you came down, I saw you
hesitate, as if this earlier you was also with us
and might stop for a while, roll another, watch
our dead dog running after his ball
but the moment passed and you kept pace with me.

Even I could see you didn't really want to be here
but you've yet to find a way of evading
the stories that spool through my head, where
walking with me on a winter afternoon can still happen
and all our griefs, all our misunderstandings
lie stranded on mud flats.

Lately you've taken to sleepwalking

turning up in our defunct caravan / the former family home / on the corner of Gloucester Road & Ashley Down & telling me you're about to move into your great-grandmother's house / you've received the letter I've yet to send you / you're off to Indonesia & don't know how long you'll be. Your hair is fair & curly / dyed a reddish brown / blonde & parted in the middle like when you were sixteen, you're wearing pyjamas & a hat that changes shape at the flick of a switch & yes, you say, this baby you're carrying in your arms, a newborn who's holding his head up already, is yours & his name is Finn.

Then there are the times you're all smiley & *are you pleased to see me?* / you wrap yourself around me, your arm around my neck / you walk straight through me. Or we're not talking, there's nothing to say / you're disagreeing with me loudly & publicly / I'm trying not to be overly excited by your being here / too busy to stop what I'm doing & listen. I watch from over the road as you bend to greet a dog the colour of Demerara sugar with long curly ears. You have a gift for me, it's a smashed chocolate rabbit wrapped in foil / I'm clutching a battered white-painted horse with a black felt shadow.

And now waves are crashing over the sandbar, silent & high as the roof of this house but you don't notice. I'm floored by the enormity of everything / you're ethereal & spangled with purple. In the field by a river a small / child / hurtles, sweat-soaked curls stuck to / their / skin & I long to go over / I don't go over / I know what happens.

What is there of you in this house

you never lived here and seldom visited in the years
after I sold the family home. Since you stopped altogether

the ash has been felled, the dog died and I've had
a new bathroom installed. The new dog's inherited

your pink towel, the one with your dead name
stitched to its edge.

Seven-year-old you smiles uneasily from a frame
on the piano. If pictures could speak, I'm not sure it would.

There's a box of keepsakes you didn't want in the attic
I kept them anyway in case one day you change your mind I

don't know maybe one day you'll change your mind.
Sometimes I let myself hope

like others might hope for a big cash prize
a respite from cancer.

**Poem for little you perched on your grandmother's pushbike
wearing a bin bag in the rain**

It's been so long since she saw you
I worry your grandmother will forget you
although I don't know why, she's forgotten
almost everything now and didn't even
recognise her Rich Tea biscuit this morning
so the moment of your passing from her mind's
likely been and gone already
without anyone noticing.

Though maybe what really troubles me is
you forgetting her, or rather
the kindness she could show when you were small
and now it's my memory I'm worrying
a too-loose ring
twisted around a shrinking finger.

When a story isn't never-ending

But I still need you, you tell your story
though even from where you're standing
at the top of the steps, you can
see the weariness in its eyes and you know
it understands what's happening.

All night you sit up with it
hoping that something will change, that the fitful
sleep that comes over it will somehow
turn things around
so that in the morning your story will leap to its feet
ready for another adventure
primed to protect you when someone runs up behind you
or says something that causes you to doubt yourself or
feel at fault, but by dawn its panting is frantic
and you lie next to it as it struggles to stay and go —
you can tell it doesn't want to leave you —
and finally you howl and it howls too
waves its tail and is gone.

And that might have been that, apart from the grief —
oh god, the grief —
but then you feel it lean against your leg
and you stretch out your hand to ruffle its fur
curl your fingers on the collar round its neck.

A betrayal

Your grandmother had no intention of dying
although she did concede that if it happened
she wouldn't mind her ashes being buried
next to Betty's in Rose Bed Number 2

but since your grandfather wanted his
scattered from the top of Hay Tor
and your aunt was adamant they should be together
that's where I took them. I remember

it was early Christmas morning
and my wish was for frost and light
with perhaps a breeze or at least some respite
from the unrelenting rain so I could maybe

channel her to the coast with the hope she might
mingle with the sand on the beach
where she loved to swelter in the sun
but as we passed the turning to Manaton

a mist came down. It's not safe to go up there
I told your brother, so we huddled at the foot, shook
out their ashes, watched them
billow over gorse and granite and out of sight.

On a nearby boulder a rose was rotting
and your brother went climbing anyway
whooping and hopping from rock
to rock in thickening fog.

When I wonder how you're living now

And then there the days I'm back in the hole I dug on the beach, buttressing a wall of red sand against the tide & my mother's saying she'll never get my socks white again only I'm the mother now & you're sixteen & the red is Anna Karenina's blood, the tide your outraged tears even though no one ever reads that book to be surprised by its ending & I'm reminded of the time you shocked the consultant endocrinologist by injecting insulin straight into the back of your leg because you'd seen your father do it so many times & from that afternoon onwards you'd have to as well & I couldn't do it for you / instead of you / I'd failed in my task which was to protect you & now the tide's running darker & I must dig deeper, remember when you told your tutor the black choker you were wearing was school uniform actually as you'd made it from a pair of old tights, back to when you were a dog called Timmy that barked & refused to answer to your name, & you were the new pupil in Year 3 playing the piano by ear in assembly, & announcing to our lodger from your pushchair That's a bakery, you can buy cake in there if you like & maybe you are / will be OK but the wall's caving in the tide breaks through it always has to.

If a story falls in a forest

When the oldest, longest-running
plotline in our story came to its close, I felt the ground
leap like the night there was that small

earthquake while we were sleeping
and something fell from the top of the wardrobe
with a bang only this time it was more like

an oak toppling, its jays and squirrels scattering,
acorns rolling out of reach, none of which
you appeared to notice. So now I can't help

wondering whether trees can fall silently after all
their tenants having long departed
in this season of scant mast.

It's a girl

And as if that wasn't enough, your grandmother gets on the bus at the top of Pigsty Hill, which is odd since she's dead, but here she is all the same, sidling down the aisle to take her seat next to me and unclasping her purse, as if she still expects the conductor to issue her with a ticket printed on that thick yellow paper that fluffs up when you rub it and rub it between your finger and thumb. Though not as odd as what she says, which might have been sorry for the disappointment that coloured everything after the midwife glanced between my legs and gave her the dreadful news, it wasn't fair to blame me, she sees that now, in fact, in her newly translated state of being, or rather, un-being, she sees all her missteps and errors so clearly but no, it's this: Tell her — yes, she does still use this pronoun for you — tell that daughter of yours she's no different from either one of us.

The dead are happy being dead

He's at least twenty-five years younger than when he
died & as we meet on the doorstep, he kisses me on the
mouth & I say Leonard, why didn't you come & find me
when you were alive? He laughs, reminds me of how far
he had to travel, all those songs he had to write &
anyway he's here now, isn't he? & we head inside to a
room with a leather settee, a bottle of Château Latour &
two wine glasses. We're just sinking into the cushions
when a shadow passes on the other side of the window &
we duck down out of sight, but it's too late, she's spotted
us & — this is strange — she's radiant, your grandmother, in fact, I'm astounded to see how being dead
suits her. She has a question, though, which she mouths
through the glass, it's have you heard from her? & I look
at Leonard & look at the wine & say no, Mum, we need
to give them more time & she tuts, says yes, you always
say that, but how do you know that's what you've got?

You're not dead to me

even though your ghost is always
at my shoulder.

The dead are apt to make demands
they tell me what to do, what I am.

Even the ones that are benign have seeds
that need planting, apples waiting to be picked.

You're not as insistent as they are
you lack their substance.

You're changing all the time
though I can't see you.

One day I'll meet you in my head
and fail to know you.

It's hard feeling hopeless when everything's beautiful

This is the season when people step into
space and fall, or fall

short. Others fall asleep hoping not to wake up.
You've considered these possibilities

listened to the song of your longing
for it all to be over, for what might be peace

but these moments aren't as real
as those that hold your child, wearing a jumper

you knitted, who's explaining how
when they grow up, they'll cut a hole in the fence

between the houses you'll be living in
so you can crawl through to visit them

or skipping to the post box on their own
for the first time while you watch from the gate

and later learning the saxophone / giving up
learning the saxophone / instructing you to sell it / asking

where is it? they need it back, none of which
(apart from the sax) are gone for good.

Or is hope the albatross?

Yes, love's feathers are heavy
and sometimes you stagger under the load

but you'll never unknot it and let it go,
love is the ballast that steadies your life and besides

what's a dung beetle
freed from the burden of its dung ball?

But the weight of hope
around your neck

risks dragging you down with its blather,
its failure to deliver

so why not cut it loose, let it
spiral and founder

let frilled sharks and anglerfish startle and gawp
at this monstrous intruder.

**Why a story is more like permafrost in a time
of climate change than a tablecloth**

It would be foolish
to mistake a story for a tablecloth

not that either make good parachutes
when the time comes to take that step

and you're not sure if the air will hold you up
or rip it from your fingers as you plummet.

Although this isn't a cloth
you might lay under crockery

like my great-grandmother's snowy damask
the one Grampy dropped mustard on

during Christmas dinner in 1934
it's more the type that covers

the leftover host and chalice at Communion
or an amputation in a hospital morgue

and while it is possible
to hide inconveniences under stories

the layers will melt over years
the truths poke through.

Death of a seabird

It's not an albatross, of course,
not in a city on the edge of the North Atlantic.

It's not Flying Ant Day either
even though the sound that makes me look up
over an ocean of choppy roofs
comes from gulls
an anguish of wings and shrieking
as one of their kind lands on a spike
installed to stop nesting.

I can't watch as it flaps and grapples
skewered through one side,
heaving and sliding on wet red metal.

All I can do is shut the blind it's not
an albatross.

Not the worst thing

In some ways it's worse than your child
being dead, someone says

as if rejection and the shame of explaining it
are the most terrible things that can happen to a mother

but I recall the losses that felled
friends, a cousin, my uncle

the sentence that has no words
won't be commuted.

Meanwhile I can still walk around thinking of you
or not, wondering whether I will

or won't see you again and how much that does
or doesn't matter in any moment oh don't get me

wrong, it's always winter here. And the cold strikes up
from the pavement through the worn soles of my boots

but your hands are snug in their gloves
your loved heart pumps.

Blessing

Your grandmother died the day
the devil spat on the blackberries
putting paid to that glut of jam.
As news spread, the share price of jam sugar
plummeted and the Dow Jones index closed
more than four hundred points down.

Over the next few months the exhaustion of
not being allowed to be me lumbered into flight
and disappeared over the tree tops, legs trailing.
My back stopped hurting and I found myself
contemplating taking down the front room curtains
and scrubbing the mould above the window
with a diluted solution of bleach. First though

I surveyed my ramparts of books
took the ones I won't read in the days that are left
to the second-hand bookshop and
rearranged the rest so they can breathe and oh my
child, if all this sounds familiar, if you only feel
free when free of me, take this as my blessing.

Your silence is all I have left

so I'll take it, make of it a field
tucked in the gap between factory buildings
and the railway embankment
with views over the floodplain to the river, the hills,
the high cloud mountains of another, older country.

The shouting of jackdaws and rooks in the rookery
the endless drill of motorway traffic won't break its surface
nor the bulldozers grazing empty farmland,
digging foundations for a future town
beyond wood and common.

One day a sparrowhawk will come
followed by rain that will wash the silence
clean of hope
and when I straighten up, stretch my arms, my back
I'll find I've become its hollowing oak, its fox-

trodden paths, the ditch, these stands of towering hogweed.
By autumn I'll be mist on a distant horizon
in winter I'll lie down and turn to mud
looking up at the shapes the night birds make
against the dark.

The counsel of hares

And maybe someday in late December
you'll glance through an unlit window

see us walking down the street
past factories and workshops

empty car lots
disappearing in the dusk

and a path that holds no play of light
only a field at its end and a circle of watchful hares

with us transfixed in the act of witnessing
something uncanny, not intended for us to see.

And maybe whole lives pass as we hold our breath
before we turn, retrace our steps

just as you might retrace our steps
as you stand at that window.

I'll no longer be with you
trapped as I am in these years in between

recalling too late how time hurries on
leaves us beyond it

how even on days with no light in them
wonders might happen.

Notes

Dedication   Wisdom the albatross is a wild female Laysan albatross, the oldest confirmed wild bird in the world. She is believed to have raised up to 36 chicks, and to have flown over 3 million miles while foraging for them.

Page 15   **No protocols can save me now**   The title of this poem comes from Eric Sofge's article 'What Happens If An Astronaut Floats Off In Space?', which originally appeared in the October 2013 issue of Popular Science.

Page 22   **Once we were birds**   In mediaeval legend, it was said the female pelican pecked her breast to feed her young with her blood during times of famine, thus symbolising the self-sacrificial aspect of motherhood.

Page 27   **What the currents of the Skagerrak taught me**   The Skagerrak is a strait running between the Jutland peninsula of Denmark, the southeast coast of Norway and the west coast of Sweden. Frederikshavn is a port on the north-east coast of Denmark.

Page 34   **Disappointment is a sedimentary rock**   Naked mole-rats live in colonies in which only one female – the Queen – breeds, and the majority of workers (both males and females) spend their entire lives supporting the colony.

Page 50   **Radio silence**   During the superheated re-entry through the Earth's atmosphere of the Apollo 13 Command Module, radio blackout lasted 87 seconds longer than anticipated.

Page 53 **Conversations with Silence iii** In 'The Magician's Nephew' by C S Lewis, Digory Kirke rang the Charn bell, whose continuous sweet note grew so loud, it caused walls to crumble and awakened Jadis, the evil Queen of Charn and, later, Narnia.

Page 74 **Blessing** In folklore, the Devil is said to spit on any unpicked blackberries on Michaelmas Day, rendering them inedible from this time onwards.

Page 75 **Your silence is all I have left** After Rumi (1207-1273): 'Out beyond ideas of wrongdoing and rightdoing there is a field. I'll meet you there.'

Page 76 **The counsel of hares** Assemblies of up to forty hares in a rough circle with two or three in the centre are called 'parliaments' or 'counsels'. Rarely encountered, their purpose is unknown.

Also by Deborah Harvey

Communion (poetry), 2011
Map Reading For Beginners (poetry), 2014
Breadcrumbs (poetry), 2016
The Shadow Factory (poetry), 2019
Learning Finity (poetry), 2022

Dart (fiction), 2013

Indigo Dreams Publishing Ltd
24, Forest Houses
Cookworthy Moor
Halwill
Beaworthy
Devon
EX21 5UU
www.indigodreamspublishing.com